NEPTUNE

PLANETS IN OUR SOLAR SYSTEM

CHILDREN'S ASTRONOMY EDITION

SPEEDY
PUBLISHING

Speedy Publishing LLC
40 E. Main St. #1156
Newark, DE 19711
www.speedypublishing.com

Neptune is the eighth
and farthest planet
from the Sun.

Neptune is the fourth largest planet in the solar system.

Neptune is 17 times the mass of Earth.

The atmosphere of Neptune is made of hydrogen and helium, with some methane.

Neptune is the
most dense
among the
giant planets
in the Solar
System.

It is the coldest planet
in the Solar System.

Neptune is
a gas giant,
meaning that
its surface is
gas rather
than a hard
rocky surface
like earth.

The discovery of Neptune
was one of the most
exciting discoveries
in astronomy.

Neptune's atmosphere gives it a blue color which is fitting with it being named after the Roman god of the sea.

Neptune was the
first planet found
by mathematical
prediction.

Neptune has 14 known moons. Triton is the largest Neptunian moon.

Neptune was first seen in 1846 from the observatory in Berlin.

Neptune has
a planetary
ring system.
The rings may
consist of ice
particles.

Neptune's magnetic field is 27 times stronger than Earth's.

Neptune completes its orbit around the Sun every 164.79 Earth years.

Neptune suffers the most violent weather in our Solar System.

The average distance between Neptune and the Sun is 4.50 billion kilometers.

Neptune has a diameter of 30,598 miles, almost 4 times the diameter of Earth.

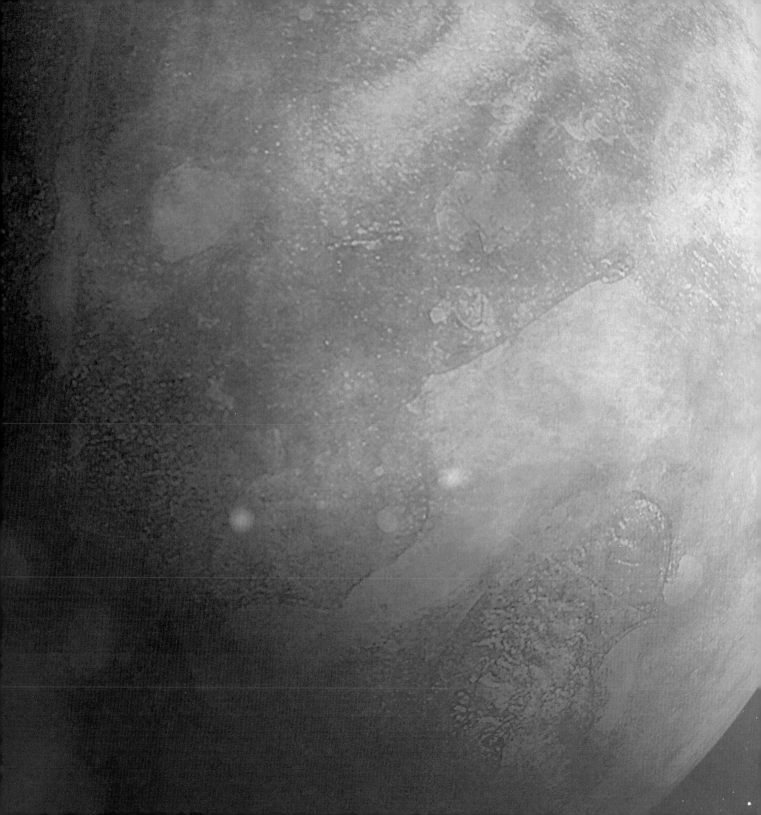

Neptune's
rotation period
is roughly
16.11 hours.

In 1989, the Voyager
2 spacecraft swept
past the planet.

Made in United States
North Haven, CT
14 March 2023

34060459R00024